Ancient Magick for Today's Witch Series

HERB MAGICK

MONIQUE JOINER SIEDLAK

OSHUN
PUBLICATIONS
oshunpublications.com

Cover Design by MJS

Cover Images by MidJourney

Published by Oshun Publications

www.oshunpublications.com

Ancient Magick for Today's Witch Series

The *Ancient Magick for Today's Witch Series* is a series for modern witches to explore ancient magick, covering Celtic, Gypsy, and Crystal magic, among others. It offers practical advice on spells, rituals, and enchantments for today's use, incorporating natural energies and spiritual connections. With insights into Shamanism, Wicca, and more, it helps readers enhance their magickal journey, offering paths to protection, prosperity, and spiritual growth by combining ancient wisdom with contemporary practice.

Wiccan Basics
Candle Magick
Wiccan Spells
Love Spells
Abundance Spells
Herb Magick
Moon Magick
Creating Your Own Spells
Gypsy Magic
Protection Magick
Celtic Magick

Shamanic Magick
Crystal Magic
Sacred Spaces
Solitary Witchcraft
Novice Witch's Guide

MONIQUE JOINER SIEDLAK
GET UPDATES, FREEBIES & GIVEAWAYS
JOIN MY NEWSLETTER
MOJOSIEDLAK.COM/MOONLIGHT-MUSINGS

Contents

Introduction

Merry Meet!

Herbs have been an indispensable part of human existence for tens of thousands of years, not only as nourishment and medicine but also as part of our spiritual practice. Herbs were used to commune with the spirits or induce the user into a trance state, among other things. As an active spiritual practice, Wicca relies as much on herbs today as early people did thousands of years ago.

Herbs are so versatile and can be found in the most unlikely of places. What may seem like a weed or pest to the average person is actually a valuable, irreplaceable part of a person's spiritual practice and highly revered.

Wicca is no different in this regard, and in the following pages, we will discover the varied purposes and uses of herbs and where to find them and what to do with the herbs once you have them. Wicca alone is a fantastic journey of discovery, education, and growth. While the use of herbs in Wicca may only be a fraction of what Wicca is overall, we hope you will enjoy this book and its contents as much as we enjoyed putting it together.

ONE

Using Herbs in Magick

HERBS HAVE BEEN A PART OF HUMAN EXISTENCE FOR POSSIBLY as long as 60,000 years. A Paleolithic burial site in Iraq yielded eight different plant pollens, seven of which are now used as medicine. This indicates that we have been using herbs since the beginning of our time here on Earth. Evidence of herbs used by prehistoric people was found in Europe, among the possessions of the Ötzi man who had been frozen in the Ötztal Alps for 5000 years. The Sumerians were the first to record the study of medicinal plants. Five thousand years ago, they recorded hundreds of herbs with medicinal properties on clay tablets. While 3500 years ago, the ancient Egyptians compiled the Ebers Papyrus, a list of about 850 medicinal plants, including garlic, juniper, and cannabis. We would assume that ancient peoples had no knowledge of medicine per se, so were these herbs' healing effects considered magic?

Wicca is a modern spiritual practice, having only been brought into existence in the late 19th century. However, magick has been with us for thousands of years, and the original medicine man of ancient peoples, the shaman, was more of a magician than a doctor. Along with spells and talismans, herbs were used to affect the work of the ancient magician significantly. The more modern Wiccan practices magick, and while we live in the 21st century, our use of herbs in this practice is not much different from the shamanic traditions of ancient peoples all over the world. In fact, we may be closer to them in our use of herbs than we realize.

Anthropologists observed that these different cultures throughout the world all had one thing in common. They revered plants and indeed believed the plants themselves were supernatural, holding power within their very roots, stems, and petals. In the Americas, Africa, Europe, and Asia, the plants' magical properties were strongly connected with the ritual practice. For example, the Surinamese Winti religion, a magickal practice, has an impressive array of magickal herbs associated with different deities, purposes, and effects. Most of their magickal herbs were from a particular group of plants native to Suriname and were used to heal sicknesses or commune with the dead. Those individual plants were considered magical today because they had some connection to the modern user's immigrant past. In this way, we can maintain that the use of herbs in modern Wicca is dependent on what our ancestors did with the herbs in their practices.

Herbs, as instruments in Wicca, are very versatile. They may be used in many ways, including but not limited to teas, tinctures, baths, rubs, oils, and smudges and even smoked. We will focus on merely a few of those methods, namely, teas, baths, oils, and smudges. However, as herbs are versatile, we also encourage you to experiment with herbs in your Magickal practice and grow in the knowledge of the sacred plants.

TWO

Ways to Use Herbs

HERBS ARE COMPLICATED LITTLE BEINGS WITH THEIR OWN
characteristics, genders, planets, and elements coming into
one. Herbs are often sacred to a certain God, Goddess, or
deity. In Wicca, we call this correspondence, and it is an essential factor in the use of herbs in spells and rituals as it tells us
which herbs to use in which way and to what end.

One of the most straightforward methods to use herbs is
as a charm. You will put a particular herb into a small cloth
bag and carry it with you or place it where its power is
needed. This will differ according to the spell you are
performing.

Tea is another simple way to use herbs in Wicca. The herb
will be boiled or steeped in hot water and drunk. Some herbs
like valerian can alter consciousness or induce a trance-like
state. Be sure of what herbs you are ingesting and what the
effects may be as you wouldn't want to poison yourself unin-
tentionally.

Baths are a relaxing way to use herbs. You will put the
herbs whole or in a cloth bag into your warm bath water and
soak yourself or an item in the bath. Herbs can be used in a

bath to assist with external conditions like eczema or psoriasis or simply to induce relaxation.

Making herbal essential oils can be slightly more complicated as it may require the use of equipment such as a still, but simple herbal oil can be made by steeping the herbs in an oil base for a few days. These oils can be used in Wiccan practice for anointing people and items, being heated in a diffuser, or even placed into food.

Lastly, herbs can be burned as an incense or smudge, which is more commonly done to clear energies from a space or object such as when a Wiccan burns white sage.

Teas

Making herbal tea is one of the most natural things you can do in terms of Wiccan practice. Many different herbs decoct or extract by boiling with hot water very well, and their uses vary greatly. From yarrow tea to mint tea, there is a herbal tea for all Wiccan requirements.

As tea is taken orally, as a drink, it is usually used in a medicinal way to cure or ease ailments of the body and mind. However, in some instances, tea can be used to induce an altered state of consciousness.

We will look at a few different herbal teas and their uses.

Yarrow tea is a prevalent herbal tea used in witchcraft. It can help intensify the properties of other herbs. It is said to expel toxins from the body and, therefore, be taken when feeling ill or flu-ish. Yarrow tea drunk before divination can make you more conscious and increase the power of your clairvoyance. Also, yarrow tea will stop aches and pains due to cold weather. Steep the fresh yarrow in hot water with a fresh mint sprig for five minutes and drink while hot.

Thyme is a wonderfully versatile herb used in many different cultures and for many distinct purposes. As a tea for the Wiccan, it has a great many applications. It is powerful as an antiseptic, antibiotic, and as a diuretic. Its diuretic properties mean it helps eliminate toxins—steep fresh thyme in hot water and drink as a remedy for cough and indigestion. When combined with honey, it can ease a sore throat, and if taken cold, the tea can cure a headache.

Marigold, a flower found in gardens all over the world, is a potent infusion. Steeped in hot water and drunk while hot, the marigold tea can help combat symptoms of flu, fever, rheumatism, jaundice, and even severe menstrual pains.

Basil, yet another herb used worldwide for its taste and aroma, has several wonderful uses as a tea for the Wiccan herbologist. If brewed or steeped in hot water, it makes a pungent, aromatic tea, which is good for calming the nerves, settling the stomach, and easing cramps.

A strong herbal tea with magical uses is the decoction of St. John's Wort. The herb should be gathered on Midsummer's eve and cleansed in the smoke of a bonfire. Then, the cleansed herb is steeped in hot water before being drunk hot. Drinking a tea of St. John's Wort will increase your courage and willpower and is suitable for when you must take on a difficult task or break a habit or an addiction. This is definitely one powerful herbal tea.

Ginger, a universal staple in both kitchens and apothecaries, is a powerful root used for many different things. As a tea, it acts as a digestive aid or helps treat a cold. Additionally, it can be used as a tea to treat headaches or for stiffness in the joints. A potent ginger tea with multiple healing functions is made in the following way. Combine a liberal pinch of dried, ground ginger with a pinch of peppermint and a pinch of cloves. Prepare in a cup of hot water and drink it all down, feeling the natural remedy take hold.

Baths

An herbal bath can be relaxing, refreshing, and healing for any person, but it has other uses. Even in spiritual practices such as Christianity, the ritual bath is essential, symbolically washing away sins and being able to emerge from the water spiritually clean And new. It's no different for Wiccans who use baths for healing, to energize and to cleanse. Traditionally, an herbal bath will contain a decoction of herbs or even oils and used to submerge a person or object. Different herbal baths have different purposes; let's take a look at some of those purposes.

A spell bath is usually done before the Wiccan performs a spell or ritual, and the effect is that of cleansing and energizing before the performance. A basic cleansing bath will contain the following herbs, basil for psychic energy, borage for strengthening the soul body, and lavender to clear the mind, centaury a traditional magickal herb, and rue a popular herb for bathing. Fill small muslin sachets with equal amounts of the herbs place into a bath of hot water 5 minutes before you get into it. Please note that rue can be used to induce abortion and should not be handled by pregnant people.

A herb covered in the section on teas but can also be used in a bath is thyme. Used for magickal cleansing in the springtime, as part of a spring cleaning, a bath infused with thyme and marjoram will cleanse the mind, body, and soul, renewing you after the long winter and preparing you for the warm months ahead.

The orris root is a herb of feminine power, corresponding with the Mother Goddess Venus. A bath infused with orris root can increase the Wiccan's sexual appeal.

On the other end, the herb Lovage corresponds with the masculine power and the sun. Soaking oneself in a bath containing dried and powdered Lovage is cleansing and empowering for the masculine Wiccan and can increase sexual attractiveness.

Herbal baths tend to lean more toward cleansing, just as teas are for medicinal purposes, and a tub of hyssop is no different. Widely used during the Middle Ages, hyssop is still used by the modern Wiccan for cleansing and the banishment of negative energy. Bath yourself in a decoction of hyssop to banish negative energy obtained during encounters with negative people or situations.

Oils

Like herbs used in teas and baths, herbs can be used in aromatic and essential oils to treat, calm, heal, and cleanse. Many religions and spiritual practices use oils for anointing or diffusing and in rituals and spells. Oils can be applied to the skin, combined with food or used in baths. Magickal oil, like many other magickal items, has a multitude of uses. For example, you could wear it as perfume and use its magickal effects on your body. In the case of anointing, it can be used on any object imaginable, from candles and crystals to spell pouches and wands. Instead of using whole herbs in your ritual bath, you could add a few drops of the particular herbal oil instead and to the same end. When used in diffusers, you can buy specially made oil or mix some of the oil with water to be used in your diffuser or oil burner. As mentioned with baths, you can also put herbal essential oil directly onto incense coal instead of the dry herbs. Let's look at the different types of herbal oils and how and why they are used.

Patchouli, which is a powerful, aromatic herb, is associated with sensuality. When used in Wiccan practice, patchouli oil can be heated in a diffuser and is said to ground a person for them to carry out spells and incantations successfully.

Herbal oil, which helps relieve stress and cause relaxation, is that of the juniper berry. The juniper is referred to in the

Bible as the 'Broom Tree,' and the coals would be used to cleanse a lying tongue. In this way, we can say that juniper is useful for cleansing. As an oil, it should be heated in a diffuser; it creates a sense of relaxation, calm, and peace without the sedation experienced with chamomile or valerian.

Drinkers of Earl grey will be familiar with the flavor and scent of bergamot. Bergamot is a citrus type botanical, reminiscent of orange. It can be heated in a diffuser or applied to the skin in small amounts. It is used to treat depression and mental illness and help combat the ailments above in conjunction with gratitude work (being thankful for what we have) instead of focusing on what we do not have).

Frankincense may not be a herb, but it deserves mention here as it is so powerful. While Frankincense is made from tree sap, it is highly beneficial as an essential oil. According to Robi Zeck, "Frankincense deepens and slows the rhythm of the breath, providing safe passage to the inner realms of the unconscious during meditation."

Star anise is the wonderfully fragrant botanical from Asia. It is often used in cooking and has the scent and taste reminiscent of licorice. It is versatile and has multiple applications when used as an essential oil. Anise oil allows one's conscious mind to open to the unconscious, making sense of the hidden and unknown. If you are having nightmares, you can protect yourself by sprinkling a few drops of anise oil onto your pillow before bed. For a home cleansing to drive out negative energy, burn anise oil in a diffuser or oil burner. For a spirit cleansing purification bath, add anise oil liberally to your bathwater.

Smudging

Smudging, loosely defined, uses the smoke of burning plant material to cleanse energy from a building, object, or person. One will light the smudge stick or bundle of herbs and then waft the smoke over the desired target, often while chanting a mantra or holding specific thoughts. Smudging is one of the most delightful ways to use herbs in Wicca, as you get to create something from the herbs, which is your smudge stick, and then you get to use your smudge stick in a ritual. It is satisfying in itself, and besides the natural pleasure smudging brings, the method has a multitude of purposes. If you are using loose herbs to smudge, then you will also need incense charcoal onto which you will throw your herbs for burning.

The first herb we will look at in terms of smudging is the most popularly used, even by people who are not Wiccan, white sage. White sage is called Salvia Apiana and is also known as bee sage. It is indigenous to the United States and has been used for thousands of years by the Native American people. It is known to be an antimicrobial and insect repellant. It is believed that its energy is also good at warding off evil spirits as well as clearing stale and negative energy from people or places. To cleanse and renew, light your white sage smudge stick and waft the smoke over the desired object while repeating chants such as, "Cleanse my home of any energy or negativity that does not support my family and me." You can create your incantation as fits the purpose.

Cedar, along with white sage, is commonly used by Wiccans in their beginning phases. Like other smudging herbs, it should be burned in a smudge stick. It is slow-burning and can be used for more extended rituals. It is traditionally used for renewal, protection, and grounding. It can be used to smudge a new home or a person embarking on a new journey or mission.

Eucalyptus, also recognized as blue gum, is a wonderful, versatile herb with many different purposes. As a smudging herb, it is used for good health. Smudge a person or people with eucalyptus to ensure they have good health. It can also be used alongside white sage to enhance the cleansing effects of the latter.

Lavender is yet another fragrant, powerful herb that, when

burned, releases a robust scented smoke. Burn both the leaves and stems for a more potent aroma. Burn loose lavender at the end of a long day for relaxation and peace in your mind, body, and home.

Catnip, while exciting and stimulating for cats, has another effect for people. When burned in the home, it brings peace, love, and happiness. It's suitable for young couples and families, just beginning their life's journey.

Mentioned yet again, thyme as a smudge is invaluable to the creative person. When burned, it can help clear mental blocks, increase creativity, and boost one's memory and cognitive ability.

THREE

Basics of Herbal Preparation

WICCANS, AS PRACTICING HERBALISTS, CAN GIVE NEW LIFE TO what other people consider weeds. While an average person may wish to see the dandelions gone from their perfectly manicured lawn, we know that they are a significant part of the natural world and have their place and their role. The many different herbs mentioned in this work may all be commonly known to the Wiccan, but buying a herb for cooking at your local supermarket and foraging the herb yourself may affect the outcome of your magick. Although, whether you purchase or forage, if your intentions are pure and well-meaning, then we can rest assured that the desired effect will be attained. It is vital to source your herbs and botanicals from sustainable, ethical sources. Even better is to go out in nature and pick them yourself. Once you have your herbs, you will need to know what to do with them. Herbs can be cut up and dried, dried whole, preserved in airtight containers, pressed, bound with string, put into cloth bags, or kept loose in jars until it's time for them to be used. Some herbs are better used fresh, while others become more potent when dried and cured. This is all dependent on the herb itself and the tea, bath, oil, or smudge stick you are intent on using.

Either way, you will need to understand how and why. So let's begin the journey into the basics of herbal preparation.

Harvesting

You may purchase your herbs used for magickal practice from your local supermarket or greengrocer; there is nothing wrong with that. You may also have your own herb garden, tended to with intent, patience, and love. That is even better. However, in Wicca's practice, we recommend using herbs straight from the source, Mother Nature.

If you are going out into the wild to forage herbs, follow these guidelines to do it ethically and honor the Mother Goddess

- Pick herbs from plant species with an abundant population in the wild – When we are harvesting from nature, always make sure the plant is abundant not to affect its distribution, survival and the ecosystem it is a part of. Try to avoid woodland medicinal as these are often less abundant, forage for weeds and shrubs in fields and meadows as these are often more abundant and less likely to be harmed by being picked. Before you harvest a particular plant, make sure that you know about its population and any dangers it may face in its natural area. Even if a plant is abundant in an area, over foraging or human settlement can quickly destroy the population.
- Harvest non-native or invasive plant species first – When harvesting in a particular area, be sure to determine which plant species are non-native or invasive. Often, non-native plants push out other plants that are indigenous to the area. Non-native plants can also be resource hungry and will deprive

native plants of the water and nutrients they require to survive and prosper. By picking non-native and invasive plant species first, you give the indigenous flora a chance to regain its foothold in the area and thrive as intended.

- Forage in safe areas away from human activity – Like us, plants breathe in fumes emitted by cars and factories; they can also absorb pollution and toxins in the soil and groundwater. If you forage plants that have been affected by human activity, you will also be negatively affected. Make sure you harvest plants at least 30 feet from a road and far downstream of any water pollution. If you live in a city and struggle to get to remote, wild places, try to find the local community gardens and ask if you may clear out weeds and other 'undesirable' plants.

- Be a champion of the plants - No matter what you are harvesting, whether it be a pesky thistle, an abundant dandelion, or a wild rose, always treat these organisms with respect and care they deserve as they are living beings, just like you. Take only what you need and leave no trace that you were ever there. Fill in any holes you make and be sure not to disturb animals or other creatures that live in and among the plants. Bring an offering if you intend to take from nature; a handful of grain for the birds, clean water, or seeds of a locally occurring indigenous plant will ensure that you harvest with pure intent. Make sure you collect over a large area, so you don't put too much strain on one microsystem. Take your time, breathe with purpose, and be mindful of each footstep you take.

Drying

The drying of herbs is an essential step when using in Wicca. As it is not always achievable or possible to have fresh herbs on hand, drying is the best way to save and stock your herbs. Not only are dry herbs efficient, often drying increases the potency and, therefore, the efficacy of the herb. There are many different ways to dry herbs, including hanging, laying out in the sun or an oven. Some people have suggested using the microwave, but this is not suitable for Wicca as a microwave can be a damaging instrument, breaking down the plant's essence and killing its energy. We will try to use the most natural way of drying out herbs. As our herbs are going to be used in magickal practice, we need to keep the processes as natural as possible, and so we will only detail two drying methods, air drying, and solar drying.

Not all herbs are fit for drying; however, this is a list of herbs and seeds used in Wiccan practice that are suitable:

Leaves: bay, celery, dill, geranium, lemon balm, lemon verbena, Lovage, thyme, oregano, rosemary, sage, chervil, summer savory, tarragon, and marjoram.

Seeds: anise, coriander, mustard, celery, chervil, cumin, dill, fennel, and caraway.

Flowers: bee balm, chamomile, chive, dill, geranium, lavender, marigold, yarrow, rose, thyme, linden, and nasturtium.

The first and most common way to dry herbs would be with the indoor air-drying method. You should tie the herbs together by the stem and hang them upside down in a warm, dry room. Stay away from the kitchen or bathroom as dampness and humidity can hinder the drying process and cause mold to form on your herbs. An airing cupboard works well too, just make sure that there is no strong detergent or anything like perfume nearby as you don't want your herbs to absorb the scent and become unusable. For smaller sprigs or leaves, use a drying screen, mainly fine wire mesh secured to a frame and suspended. Place your herbs sprigs in the structure and leave to dry. Herbs can take anywhere from a few hours to a few days to dry properly.

The next most suitable way to dry your herbs is in the sun. If you reside in a warm, dry area, then drying your herbs in the sun is perfect! If you inhabit a humid environment, this method may not work so well. The ideal temperature and moisture levels are 100 degrees Fahrenheit, or about 38 degrees Celsius with a humidity level of not more than 60%. You can use the same drying screen for indoor air drying but place them outside instead. Bring the herbs in at night and make sure that they are not exposed to too much direct sunlight, which could also damage the herbs' integrity. If you don't have a screen, placing the herbs in a hot car will do the same job nicely.

Using Fresh Herbs

While dried herbs are the staple of kitchens, covens, and apothecaries, fresh herbs have their place. It is often not very practical to keep fresh herbs as they will deteriorate and decompose over time. However, if you have your own herb garden, here is what you can and should do with those fresh herbs concerning magickal practice.

For romance spells that use rose petals, always use fresh rose petals.

When making pouches, bags, or charms, do not use fresh herbs as they will mold and turn bitter in the pouch, possibly creating some undesired magickal effects. Also, do not throw fresh herbs on incense coal as it will burn bitter, affecting the magickal outcome.

For offerings, it can be helpful to use both fresh and dried herbs as it creates variety in the offering and increases the value thereof.

If you wish to have your own herb garden for magickal purposes, these herbs mentioned in previous sections would be the best to grow for fresh use. They are parsley, mint, dill, basil, sage, rosemary, thyme, fennel, chamomile, tarragon, lavender, catnip, St. John's Wort, bay leaves, winter savory, peppermint, lemongrass, and bergamot.

The beautiful thing about fresh herbs in magick is that because the herbs are still fresh, they are chock full of life force and can be used successfully in spells that require pure, invigorating energy. Often, the fresh herbs will need to be used in conjunction with other herbal methods. Here is an example of a spell that uses fresh herbs for added power.

Fresh Funds Money Spell

You will need:
- Five fresh basil leaves
- A clove of garlic
- A high denomination bill ($20+)
- Patchouli oil
- A box with a lid

Place the dollar bill inside the box, place the clove of garlic on top of it and chant the following incantation, "It's time to connect and combine timeless magic with fresh allure, my funds increase, and I stay secure." Cover the money and garlic with the five basil leaves, pour five drops of patchouli oil onto the leaves. Close the box and place it under your bed. Leave the box for one moon cycle, and don't tell anyone about it. You should receive a windfall or become financially stable shortly after that.

Finally, since fresh herbs are common in the culinary arts, I believe that cooking is as close to magick as any average person can get without knowing it. It goes without saying that herbs' magickal effects can be used in your cooking to significantly impact. Whatever your purpose is, whether it be to find peace, cleanse your soul, heal your body of ailments, find and use the correct fresh herb in your cooking. When adding the herb to the meal, keep the herb's intention firmly in your mind, chant a mantra suitable to the desired purpose, and eat your food, knowing that it is full of powerful herb magick, healing, cleansing and transforming you from within.

FOUR

Herbs A-C

ACACIA

For protection, psychic and spiritual improvement, money, companionable love, and friendship. Use to anoint your candles and censers and to consecrate chests or boxes that you store your ritual tools. Use in incense to help stimulate a meditative state.

Adam and Eve Root

Primarily used by lovers where one lover keeps the Eve Root and the other lover keeps the Adam Root. It's said that it keeps your lover true to you and discourages rivals. You can also carry both roots in a small bag all the time for attraction, to bring a love to you, or for a marriage proposal.

African Violet

Used for spirituality, protection, and healing. Wear in an amulet for protection. Maintain in your home to increase spirituality. It is often burned as incense during the spring Equinox Sabbat.

. . .

Agrimony

Aids in defeating fear and inner obstructions; diffusing negative emotions. Also can be used for reversing spells. Use as a wash or oil to increase the effectiveness of all forms of healing rituals. Sew into a dream pillow along with Mugwort for the best outcomes. Combats poison and evil beings.

Allspice

Money, luck, obtaining treasure and healing. Provides added strength and energy to any spells and charms. Burn crushed allspice to attract luck and money. Use in herbal baths for healing.

Almond

Money, wisdom, abundance, and prosperity. Raises the healing energy of the gods and goddesses. Offers magickal help for overcoming dependencies and addiction. Almonds are connected with Candlemas and Beltane. Carry, wear, or use as incense to attract abundance to you.

Angelica Root

Carry the root in a pouch as a protective talisman. Use in protection and exorcism incense. Add to your bath to remove hexes. Smoking the leaves can cause visions. Angelica protects you by creating a wall against negative energy, and by filling the person with positive energy. Removes curses, hexes, or spells that may have been cast against you. Can give you a blissful outlook by boosting your aura.

. . .

Anise

Used to help ward off the evil eye, find happiness, and stimulate psychic ability. Fill a sleep pillow with anise seed to prevent disturbing dreams. Use to call upon Mercury and Apollo. Wonderful for aromatherapy. Use in purification baths with bay leaves. It's said that a sprig of Anise hung on the bedpost will restore lost youth. Use in protection and meditation incenses.

Ash

Used for sea spells magick and rituals, protection from drowning, image magick, invincibility, general protection, and luck. The leaf of this plant is used for travel safety. Burning an ash log at Yule brings prosperity. Place one tablespoon of ash leaves in a bowl of water in the bedroom overnight, then toss out in the morning – it's said doing this daily will prevent illness.

Asafetida

Use for protection and banishing negativity. Be cautioned that this herb is powerful, but has an awful smell when burned.

Balm of Gilead Tears

For love, manifestations, protection, healing, de-stressing, and assisting in healing from the loss of a loved one. Use in love sachets; carry for healing, protection, and mending a broken heart. Use to dress candles for any form of magickal healing. Burn to attract spirits.

Basil

Use in love and prosperity spells. Carry with you to attract wealth. Use it in a ritual bath to bring a new love in, or to free yourself of a present one. Scatter basil over your slumbering lover to ensure their fidelity. Also used for cleansing baths. Sprinkle on your floor for protection, and burn as an exorcism incense.

Bay Leaves

Carry to ward off evil, and sprinkle or burn for exorcism. Bay leaves can be used in potions for clairvoyance, visions, and wisdom. Place beneath your pillow to encourage prophetic dreams. Add to flushing out teas and baths. Scatter on your floor, and then sweep out for protection.

Beech

Wishes, happiness and divination. Improves literary skills. Place a leaf of beech between covers of Book of Shadows to increase inspiration.

Beet

Use for love. Beet juice can be used as ink for love magick or as a substitute for blood in spells and rituals.

Belladonna

Offers protection when positioned in a secret place in the home. Place on your ritual altar to honor the gods and goddesses and to add energy to your rituals. For the healing and forgetting of past loves.

Note: Deadly poison, do not ingest.

. . .

Benzoin

Purification, prosperity, soothing tension, dispelling anger, diminishing irritability, relieving stress and anxiety, and overcoming depression. Promotes generosity and concentration. Good to burn while using the Tarot or for success in intellectual matters. Smolder for purification. An incense of benzoin, cinnamon and basil is said to attract customers to your place of business.

Birch

For protection, exorcism and purification. When a birch planted near to the home is said to protect against the evil eye, infertility, and lightning.

Blessed Thistle

Use for purification, hex-breaking, protection from evil-removes unwanted influences, particularly of malevolent intent. Strew to cleanse buildings or rooms, beneficial in healing spells. Strengthens liver function, combat hepatitis, aids memory purifies the blood stream. Good for migraine, nausea, and gallstones.

Borage

For courage and psychic powers. Float the flowers in a ritual bath to raise one's spirits. Carry or burn as an incense to increase courage and strength of character. Sprinkle an infusion of Borage around the house to ward off evil.

Burdock

Used for cleansing magick when feeling highly negative about oneself or others. Use in protection incenses and spells.

Rinse with a decoction of burdock to remove negative feelings about yourself or others.

Blackberry Leaf

A powerful herb of protection, Blackberry leaf is used in invocations to the goddess Brigit. Used to attract wealth. If interweaved into a wreath with ivy and rowan, it will keep away evil spirits. A bramble patch of blackberry leaf is said to be a favorite hiding place for the faerie folk and is often used to invoke and attract faerie spirits.

Cacao

Cacao is an aphrodisiac, a mild euphoric, and aids in healing depression. It is tremendously effective in love potions and spells. Considered to be the Aztec's Food of the Gods. As an essential offering during Day of the Dead, Cacao can be used to placate restless spirits, or attract passed loved ones during a séance.

Camellia

Brings riches and luxury, expresses gratitude. Place fresh blossoms in water on altar during ritual to attract money and prosperity. Used in traditional Chinese medicine for treating skin conditions.

Caraway

For health, love, protection, mental powers, memory, passion, and anti-theft. Prevents lover from straying when used in love spells and potions. Ideal for consecrating ritual tools. Carry to improve memory or use in dream pillows to help you to remember your dreams. Sew caraway seed into a small white bag with white thread and hide it under the mattress of a child's crib or bed to keep the child free of illness.

Carnation

Use in protection, strength, healing, enhancing magickal powers, and achieving balance. Burn to enhance creativity. Use in bath spells.

Carob

Often used as a chocolate substitute, but although the flavor is similar, the correspondences are opposite. Useful for protection and prosperity (the dried pods were once used as currency). Can be burned as an incense to attract spirit helpers and familiars, or to deter poltergeists.

Catnip

For animal magick and healing pets, increases psychic bond with animals. Use as a tea for happiness and relaxation. Can also be used during meditation, increases psychic abilities. Useful in love magick- try burning dried leaves for love wishes.

Cayenne Pepper

Use in hexes, or to break a hex. Use in love or separation spells. The fire or spark of the spirit, it adds power to any spell. Contains capsaicin, which acts as a stimulating digestive aid. Apply externally for joint pain. Aids circulation, blood pressure, and colds. Those with ulcers or chronic bowel disorders should avoid using in large quantities.

Cedar

Use in healing, purification, money, protection, love. Cedar smoke is purifying and can cure nightmares. Keep cedar in your wallet or purse to attract money, and use in money incense. Carry a small piece of cedar in wallet or near money to attract wealth. Hang in the home to protect against lightning. Use in sachets to promote calmness. It can also be used in love sachets or burned to induce psychic powers. Use to draw Earth energy and grounding.

Chamomile

For healing, love, and reducing stress. Add to a sachet or spell to increase the likelihoods of its fulfillment. Chamomile tea is also an excellent relaxer. For prosperity wishes, use as an amulet for prosperity, use to attract money. Use in incense for sleep and meditation. Aligns the body and mind for magick. Add to your bath or use to wash your face and hair to draw love. To protect children from the evil eye, Bathe children in chamomile tea useful in breaking curses cast against you.

Chicory

Improves your sense of humor and encourages a positive outlook on life. Anoint your body with chicory juice or an infusion of chicory to obtain favors from others. Place fresh flowers of chicory on your altar or burn as an incense. Burn as incense with a black skull candle to place a hex on an enemy (not recommended, remember the Law of Three!).

Cinnamon

For success, healing, psychic powers, protection, spirituality, lust, love. Burn cinnamon as an incense or use in sachets and spells for healing, money-drawing, psychic powers, and protection. Mix with frankincense, myrrh and sandalwood for a strong protection incense to be burned every day. Can be used as a male aphrodisiac. Wear in an amulet to bring passion.

Cinquefoil

An overall magickal herb which encourages memory, self-confidence, and persuasiveness. The five points of the leaf represent love, money, health, power, and wisdom. Carry, burn, or wear to possess these traits. Used for business and house blessing. Use in spells to bring protection to a friend or loved one taking a journey. Burn as an incense during divination to bring dreams of one's intended mate. It is often connected with ritual work concerning romance. Wash your hands and forehead with an infusion of this herb nine times to wash away hexes and evil spells against you. Fill an empty egg shell and keep it in the home for powerful protection from evil forces. Wrap in red flannel and hang over the bed to ward off dark spirits of the night.

Cloves

Magickal uses include Protection, exorcism, love, money, good luck. Use in incense to attract money, drive away negativity, purify, gain luck or stop gossip. Wear to attract the opposite sex or for protection. Worn or carried to repel negative energies around you, also said to protect babies in their cribs if hung over them strung together. Burn to attract riches, drive away hostile forces, and stop any gossip about you. Carry to attract the opposite sex or bring comfort during bereavement. Cleanses the aura.

Coltsfoot

Add to love sachets and use in spells for peace and tranquility. Smoke the leaves to aid in obtaining visions.

Note: Do not use if pregnant or nursing.

Copal Resin

Add to love and purification incenses. Use a piece of copal to represent the heart in poppets.

Coriander

Love, health, immortality, and protection. Tie fresh coriander with a ribbon and hang in the home to bring peace and protection. Add to love charms and spells to bring romance or use in ritual work to ease the pain of a broken love affair. Promotes peace among those who are unable to get along. Throw the seeds in lieu of rice during Handfastings and other rituals of union. Use the seeds in love sachets and spells. Add powdered seeds to wine for an effective lust potion. Wear or carry the seeds to ward off disease and migraines.

Cumin

Burn with frankincense for protection. Mix with salt and scatter to keep away evil spirits and bad luck. Use for fidelity, protection, and exorcism. Use in love spells. Steep cumin seed in wine to induce lust. Place the seeds on, in or near an object to prevent theft.

Clover, Red

Brings good luck. Protection, money, success, clairvoyance, beauty, love, fidelity, and exorcism. Encourages clairvoyant powers. Use for rituals to enhance beauty and youth.

. . .

Comfrey Leaf

A strong herb for protection against any type of negativity, especially when traveling, and particularly for protection in the astral realms. Use for efforts concerning matters relating to real estate or property, stability, and, endurance. Place some in your luggage to help prevent loss or theft. Wear for travel safety and protection. Use the root in money spells and incenses.

FIVE

Herbs D-F

Damiana

Use in lust spells, Sex magick, love, and visions. Highly useful in tantric magick, astral travel, deep meditation, and spirit quests. Use in love baths. Burn as an incense to increase visions. Damiana can be made in a tea for use in sex magick. It is a gentle aphrodisiac. Good for captivating a male lover. Utilized by solitary practitioners to open the chakras and increase their psychic abilities. This herb should be stored in a container with a quartz crystal.

Note: Internal use of this herb can be toxic to the liver.

Dandelion Leaf

For divination, wishes, and calling Spirits. Use the root in a tea to enhance psychic powers. Used in Samhain rituals. Sleep, protection, healing. Bury in northwest corner of yard to bring favorable winds. Use in sachets and charms to make wishes come true. Use to make dream pillows and sachets.

Dill

Use for money, protection, luck and lust. Used in love and protection charms. Good at keeping away dark forces, practical for house blessing. Hang in the doorway to protect your home, or carry to protect your person. Add to a ritual bath to become irresistible to the one you desire. Use in love and lust spells. Add grains of dill seed to a bath before going on a date to make you irresistible.

Dragon's Blood

To increase the potency of a spell, burn as an incense. Has a strong banishing power against negative influences and bad habits. A pinch under the mattress is believed to prevent impotency. Used as a form of magickal ink. Carry or sprinkle around the home or place of business to drive away negativity. Carry or wear for good luck.

Eucalyptus Leaf

Uses include countless healing properties. Draws protection and healing vibrations. Use to purify and cleanse any area of unwanted energies. Also useful in dream and sleep pillows.

Eyebright

Carry to bring an amusing and bright attitude when life seems dark and negative. Carry this herb to improve psychic ability, encourage levelheadedness, increase memory, and increase positive outlook.

Fennel Seed

Use for protection spells of all kinds. Healing, virility, endurance, courage, vitality and strength. Hang in windows and doors to ward off evil. Prevents curses, possession and negativity. Use for purification. Gives strength, courage and longevity.

Feverfew

A strong herb for health and spiritual healing. Include in charms or sachets for love and protection Use to fend off sickness and strengthen your immune system. Protects travelers. Keep in your suitcase or car when you travel.

Fig, Dried

Sacred to Dionysus, Juno and numerous others. A great ingredient in spell bags for divination, fertility, love. It is suggested for a Beltane altar. If placed on the doorstep before leaving it will ensure you will arrive home safely. Write a question on a fig leaf and if the leaf dries slowly, the answer is yes, otherwise the answer is no.

Flax Seed

Use to keep the peace at home. Useful in healing and protection spells. Mix seeds with red pepper and keep in a box in the home to protect it. Place flax seed in a bowl to absorb negative energy. Put in a sachet to protect against hostile magick. Place some in shoe or in pocket, wallet, purse, or altar jar with a few coins to ward off poverty. An infusion made with flax seed sprinkled around the area before divination can give a more accurate reading of someone's future. Burn flax seed for divinatory powers. Also, carry in your wallet or purse to attract money.

Frankincense Resin

Used as an offering at Beltane, Lammas, and Yule. For

ventures, cleansing, purification. Burn for protective work, consecration, and meditation. Enhances the power of topaz. Use in rituals and magick associated with self-will, self-control, or the ego. Embodies the ability of the divine to move into manifestation. Add to charm bags and sachets to bring success. Mix with Cumin and burn as incense for powerful protection.

SIX

Herbs G-J

GALANGAL ROOT

For courage, strength, and for avoiding legal problems. Also psychic abilities, luck, money. It is worn or carried and protects its owner and draws good luck. Placed in a leather sachet with silver, it brings money to the wearer. To break spells and curses, burn powdered galangal. To promote lust, carried or sprinkled around your home. When worn as a talisman, galangal helps psychic development and protects the owner's health. Use caution with this plant.

Gardenia

Carry or wear to attract love or friendship. Promotes peace and protection from outside forces. When burned with dried flowers in healing incenses and mixtures, it can bring peace and comfort to someone who is ill. Sprinkle around a room to bring tranquil feelings.

Garlic

Use is in protection spells, garlic is traditionally used to ward off vampires. Its enormous healing properties, antifungal, antiviral, and strengthening.

Rubbing fresh, peeled garlic against ailing body parts then throw the garlic into running water is believed to absorb diseases.

Ginger

Promotes sensuality, sexuality, personal confidence, prosperity, and success. Attracts ventures and new practices. Eat before performing spells to increase your power. Adds to the strength and speed of any mixture of which it is a part. Place in charm bag, amulet, or medicine bag to increase good health and protection. For the consecration of your athame, use in herbal mixtures to strengthen and energize the ritual blade. It's said that a ginger root in the form of a human is a very powerful magickal token.

Ginseng Powder

Use the root in spells to attract love, maintain health, draw money and ensure sexual potency. Carry to enhance beauty. For transformation, endurance and sexual potency. Burn as incense to break curses or ward off evil spirits.

Hazel

For wishes, luck, fertility, protection, and guards against being struck by lightning. Carry to ease grief over a lost love. Use in a sachet to reduce passions. Use in love spells and spells to ward off evil. Hazel is an ancient Celtic tree of wisdom, inspiration, and poetry. Hazel nuts are eaten before divination. Wands of hazel represent white magic and healing, while the forked sticks are used to as a dowsing rod to find water or even buried treasure. To solicit the assistance of plant fairies, string hazelnuts on a cord and hang up in your house, altar or ceremonial room. The leaves have also served as a tobacco substitute.

Heather

For luck, protection, and immortality. Dip heather in water and sprinkle it about in a circle to bring about rain. Carry in charms or sachets to protect against violent crimes. Use in decorations around your home to encourage peace.

Hibiscus Flower

Useful as an aphrodisiac and in love spells. Also use to induce dreams, and enhance psychic ability and divination. Soothes nerves, antispasmodic. Tea aids digestion, and sweetens breath. Helpful with itchy skin.

High John

The uses of High John include confidence, strength, conquering any situation, obtaining success, winning at gambling, luck, money, love, health, and protection. High John is also known as a multiuse herb. Useful in all ritual work associated to prosperity. Wash your hands in a brew of the herb before participating in games of chance.

Holly Leaf

An excellent protective herb for luck and dream magick. Also keeps away lightning, poison, evil spirits, and other negative forces. The wood is used for all magickal tools as it will enhance any wish you have.

Note: For ritual use only, do not consume.

. . .

Honeysuckle

Draws quick abundance, money, and success. Assists confidence, articulateness and, sharpens your intuition. Use honeysuckle in charms and sachets to attract money or circle green candles with honeysuckle flowers. To increase psychic powers mash the flowers and rub into your forehead.

Hops

Place inside pillow to bring about sleep. Burn in healing incenses and spells. Use in healing charms, sachets and amulets. Drink tea after magickal practices to shift your energy back to everyday existence.

Horehound

Used as a tea to increase concentration, focus energy and strength. Carry with you or burn for protection and excellent for blessing your home. To keep your home free from negative forces, gather flowering Horehound and tie with a ribbon and hang in your home.

Hyssop

The most commonly used purification herb in magick. Lifts vibrations and promotes spiritual opening; an excellent purifying herb. Use in purification baths and spells.

Ivy

Protects the homes it grows about and over from evil and harm. An ivy plant hanging in front of the home will repel negative influence and discourage unwanted guests. When mix in a sachet with Holly as a wedding gift, it provides protection to the newly married couple. To discover if anyone is working negative magick against you. Place ground ivy around the base of a yellow candle on a Tuesday, then burn the candle.

Jasmine

Use in sachets and spells to attract spiritual love and attract a soul mate. To draw wealth and money, carry or burn the flowers. To induce sleep or burn in the bedroom or use in dream pillows to bring prophetic dreams. Aids in promoting new and inventive ideas.

Job's Tears

For luck in wishes, obtaining job, and blessings. Used in numerical of three or seven in mojo and charm bags to draw luck, wishes and money to you. Seven tears are used in a seven day magic spell to grant a wish. For wishing magick, make a wish while holding seven seeds, then throw them into running water Three Job's tears ought to be carried for good luck.

Juniper Berries

Makes a good incense to be used for protection. It can be burned or carried to enhance psychic powers. Draws good, healthy energies and love. Banishes energies harmful to your good health. Use juniper oil in your magickal workings to increase money and prosperity.

SEVEN

Herbs K-M

LAVENDER

Uses include love, healing, sleep, purification, protection, and peace. Supports healing from depression. Excellent in sleep pillows and bath spells. To induce sleep and rest, burn the flowers then scatter the ashes around the home to bring peace and harmony. Use in love spells and sachets.

Lemon

Used in purification, cleansing, spiritual opening, and elimination of obstacles. To love sachets and mixtures add dried lemon peel

Lemon Balm

For healing, love, success, and psychic/spiritual development. Use in love charms and spells to pull towards you a partner.

Lemon Verbena

Use as love charms, youth, beauty and attractiveness to the opposite sex. Use in cleansing baths and rituals before working magick. Bury in the yard or keep in the home to encourage wealth, protect from lightning and storms, and bring peace. Wear around your neck or place under a pillow to prevent bad dreams.

Lemongrass

A popular herb to work with for magickal purposes in both Hoodoo and Mexican Folk Magic traditions. As a double-sided herb, lemongrass will stimulate psychic awareness and is also used for personal purification on the one hand calming, good for deepening meditation or trance. It has also been used by some as a hexing herb mainly intended at making someone's life difficult and full of complications. You can also make lemongrass into a tea and add it to your regular floor wash to get rid of jinxes and enemy tricks placed on your door-step.

Lilac

When you are considering a short romantic fling, this is the flower you want. Use in spells where a love affair is desired without the objective of a long-term or serious relationship. Plant lilac bushes around your property to protect it and keep away. Also helpful for psychic power in general.

Lovage

Add the powdered root to cleansing and purification baths to release negativity. Carry in a sachet or charm on your person to attract love.

• • •

Mandrake Root

Mandrake strengthens the magick of any spell. Sleep with it for three nights during the full moon to charge the mandrake root with your own personal power. A whole mandrake root placed in the home will bring protection and prosperity. Carried on you, it will attract love and courage. As a hallucinogen it has great power as a visionary herb, when used in tea empowering your visions and pushing them into manifestation.

Marigold

Provides good luck in court and other legal matters. Add an infusion of marigold to your bath for five days to find "Mr. Right". To attract new love or add life to your current relationship Add to sachets, incense and amulets. Place above the bed or in dream pillows for prophetic dreams. Scatter under the bed for protection while sleeping.

Meadowsweet

To increase the chances of getting a job, use meadowsweet. Aids you during times of distress. During love magick, use as an altar offering. Burn or spread about the house to get rid of disharmony in the home or remove tensions. Carry to gain popularity and friendship.

Mint

Use dried leaves to fill a green poppet for healing. To bring wealth and prosperity, place in your wallet or purse or rub on some money. It stimulates energy, vitality, and communication. Can draw customers to your business. To draw good spirits to assist in your magick, use on your altar. Place in your home for protection.

. . .

Mistletoe

For protection from lightning and fire, hang in the home. Wear in an amulet of mistletoe to protect against unwanted advances, drive back negativity and ill will. Take with you for luck in hunting. Use to draw in customers, money and business. For healing, use in ritual baths or prayer bowls.

Note: Poisonous, use with caution.

Morning Glory Blossoms

Thought to be sacred to the Aztecs. Place under your pillow to stop nightmares and induce beneficial psychic dreams. Used for binding, banishing, and promoting attraction to someone or something. To banish someone, wrap the vine around a poppet nine times. Remember the law of three. Not suggested for use in any negative magick.

Note: Do not consume as it's toxic. Poisonous, use with caution.

Moss

Use in "Witch Bottles" for home and business. For women, place in your bra when a male lover is near to attract sexual attention. Carry any type of moss removed from a gravestone to ensure good luck, particularly with money. Use in prosperity spells, spells to Mother Earth, and Gnome magick.

Mugwort

Drink as a tea sweetened with honey before divination. The plain tea can also be used to wash crystal balls and magick mirrors. Burn with sandalwood or wormwood in scrying rituals. Use in dream pillows for prophetic dreams.

Leaves of mugwort can be placed around these to aid in scrying.

Mullein

For protection and courage while sleeping. Useful in protection and exorcism spells. Use on scrying tools to aid divination and summon spirits. Considered to be the original Witch's torch, as it is used to light spells and rites.

Mustard Seed

Commonly used in Voodoo charms. To guard against injury carry a few grains in a small bag. Scatter red mustard seed around your house to ward off burglars. One of the oldest known good luck amulets is to use yellow mustard seed in an amulet to bring faith and success.

Myrrh

Burn as a powerful incense to bring peace and for consecration, and blessing of charms, talismans, and magickal tools. This herb has a high psychic vibration that will intensify any magickal working. Increases the power of any incense of which it is a part of. Typically, it's burned with Frankincense.

Myrtle

Sacred to the Goddess Venus, myrtle has been used in love charms and spells all through history. Grow indoors for good luck. To attract love, carry or wear myrtle leaves. It's said that charms made of the wood have special magickal properties. While making love charms, potions or during rituals for love wear fresh myrtle leaves.

EIGHT

Herbs N-R

NETTLES

Carry to remove a curse and send it back, or sprinkle around the house to keep out evil. Use in purification baths. Use with a poppet or carry in a sachet to send back a spell to the one who cast it.

Nutmeg

Carry nutmeg for good luck, and to increase psychic powers. Use in money and prosperity spells. On green candles for prosperity, sprinkle nutmeg powder. It is a hallucinogen when made into a tea and is very toxic in large doses. Use no more than a pinch.

Orange

Attracts abundance and happiness through love and marriage. Focus on a yes or no question while you eat an orange, and then count the seeds. The number of seeds will give you the answer. An even number of seeds and the answer is no, an odd number of seeds is yes. You can use the leaves and flowers in love rituals to bring on a marriage proposal. Adding an infusion of orange to your bath to increase desirability and beauty.

Orange Bergamot

Carry in a sachet while gambling to draw luck and money. Very powerful for attracting success. To increase its power, burn at any ritual.

Orris Root

The main use of orris root is to find and hold love. The powder made from the root is used as a love drawing powder. Gives protection from evil spirits. For personal protection, the roots and leaves are hung in the house and added to your bath.

Patchouli

For money and love use in spells, sachets, baths and mixtures. Place in your wallet or purse to draw money. For fertility, place in a charm or use in incense. Helps to ground you and bring your awareness back to the physical level. Burn to bring about business growth.

Pau D`Arco

Can be made powerful by drawing down the waning Moon directly into the herb. It is well matched for ritual healing or for empowering remedies to ward off negativity.

Passion Flower

Stimulates emotional balance, peace, attracts friendship

and prosperity. Increases the sexual drive, as it is used in love spells. Calming and soothing, encourages emotional balance, aid in sleep.

Pennyroyal

To attract money and to aid in business transactions, carry in a green bag. Burn for protection during meditation and astral travel. Carry when dealing with negative vibrations of all kinds and use for ridding negative thoughts against you.

Peppermint

Use to increase the atmosphere of an area or in spells and incense for healing and purification. To ensure peaceful night sleep and bring about prophetic dreams, place in a sleep pillow. Burn peppermint in a new home to clear out any illness and negative energy and anoint your furnishings and household items with peppermint oil. Use in magickal workings to deliver the push needed to bring change to your life. Carry with other herbs to increase love and abundance wishes.

Pine

Burn for strength, and to reverse negative energies as it encourages clean breaks, success, strength, grounding, new beginnings, prosperity, and growth. The scent of pine is useful in the easing of guilt and dedicated wisdom.

Raspberry Leaf

For calming, stimulates sleep and visions. Used for protection, healing, and love. To keep your current love relationship alive, bathe in an infusion of raspberry.

. . .

Rose Petals

Use in love spells of all kinds. Drink rose tea before bed for prophetic dreams. Excellent for use in incense, potpourri or bath magick for healing, luck, protection. Promotes joy of giving, domestic peace and happiness.

Rose Hips

The hips are strung like beads and worn to attract love. Used in healing spells and mixtures, brings good luck, calls in good spirits

Rosemary

Burn rosemary to exorcise, purify and cleanse. Use in love and lust incenses and potions. Wash hands before any healing magick with an infusion of rosemary. Use in bath magick for purification and protection. Rosemary is associated with faeries. Also for healing of all kinds.

Rue

Magickal uses include healing, health, mental powers, freedom and protection against the evil eye. Use a bundle of the fresh herbs to cast salt water for purification of the circle or removing negativity from the home. By hanging the dried herb indoors, it will help you see and understand your mistakes. Burn to drive out negativity or bad habits. Add to your incenses and poppets to prevent illness and/or speed recovery. To break hexes and curses that may have been placed against you, add to baths.

Note: Rue should not be handled by women who are pregnant.

NINE

Herbs S-Z

SAGE

Used for self-purification and dealing with grief and loss. Carried to improve mental ability and bring wisdom. Used in healing sachets and incense. Promotes emotional, spiritual, mental, and physical health and endurance. Use as incense during sacred rituals by smudging the smoke to the four corners of a room to keep away and rid negative energies and influences. It's especially beneficial when moving into a new home as it removes negative energy. Place near a personal item of a person who is ailing when performing healing spells or rituals. Write a wish on a sage leaf and place it under your pillow for three nights. If you dream of your wish, then it will come true. If you don't dream of your wish then bury the leaf in the ground so that no evil will come to you. For use in healing and money spells.

Sandalwood

Scattering sandalwood powder around your home helps clear it of negativity. Burn during spells involving protection, healing, and exorcism. The wood is excellent for healing wands. Write your wish on a chip of sandalwood and burn it in the censer or cauldron while visualizing your wish to make it come true. Helps in healing by aligning the chakras for better energy flow. Good for meditation, healing, and manifestation. Assists you in concentration.

Scotch Broom Leaf

Considered to be a Druid sacred tree. It is use in purification and protection spells. Scatter about to exorcise evil spirits. To calm the wind, burn. The branches are used to make traditional besoms which are type of broom usually associated with witches, and are one of the tools commonly used in the practice of modern Wicca. The tea can induce psychic powers, and its smoke is a sedative.

Note: Use in moderation, can be toxic.

Seaweed

Summons sea spirits and sea winds and offers protection to those at sea. Used in sachets and spells to increase psychic powers. To attract customers and bring in positive energy scrub floors and doors of your business with seaweed infusion. To use in money spells, fill a small jar with whiskey, add seaweed, capping tightly and place in your kitchen window. This will assure a steady flow of money into the household.

Spanish Moss

To maintain good luck, especially with gambling, carry Spanish moss. Use in Witch Bottle for your home and business. Place around home, or burn to banish poltergeists.

St. John's Wort

Considered to be a Druid sacred herb which is used in protection, exorcism spells and incenses of all kinds. Use the leaves in a necklace to fend off sickness and tension. Carry on your person to strengthen your courage and conviction. Burn to banish negative thoughts and energies you may have. To induce prophetic, romantic dreams placed under pillow. Protects against all forms of black witchcraft. Place in a jar in a window or burn in a fireplace to protect from fire, lightning and evil spirits. Used in divination for the care of crystals.

Note: Can be poisonous, use with caution.

Star Anise

Protections, purification, youth, psychic powers, luck. Use for protection, meditation and psychic power incenses. Can be used in purification baths. Wards off evil and averts the evil eye. A pillow stuffed with anise seeds will keep away nightmares. The tree is planted by the Japanese around temples and on graves as an herb of consecration and protection. Burned as incense to increase psychic awareness and abilities, and are also worn as beads for the same purpose. Placed on the altar to increase the power generated; one is placed to each of the four directions. Carried to bring luck, and the seeds make excellent pendulums. The tree is often grown near Buddhist temples where it is revered.

Tea

The leaves can be used in money sachets, incenses, scrying and spells. Use in talismans for courage or strength. Use as a base for lust drinks. To ensure future riches, burn the leaves.

Tobacco Leaf

Sacred to the Native American Tradition. To create

tobacco ties, bind tobacco leaves in pieces of yellow, white, red and black cloth, and hang them about the ceremonial space at the four principal directions. Smoke to accept communication with spirits. Burn as an incense to purify a space. Spirits welcome gifts of tobacco. Promotes peace, personal strength and confidence, and. Can also be used for banishing. To win a court case, mix with salt and burn with a black candle.

Thistle Flower

Can be burned as incense for protection, to bring spiritual, financial blessings and to counteract hexing. For joy, energy, vitality, and protection carry in an amulet. Use in sachet or amulet to aid in speedy recovery from surgery or illness. Hang in the home to ward off thieves and unwanted visitors.

Thyme

Burn for good health and use in healing spells and burn as purification incense. Wear to increase your psychic powers. Said to attract loyalty, fondness, and the good opinion of others. To ward off unbearable grief or provide strength and courage when needed, wear a sprig of thyme. Burn or hang in your home for banishing, purification, and to attract good health for all occupants. Use in cleansing baths prior to working candle magick. Use in dream pillows to ward off nightmares and ensure restful sleep. To ensure a constant flow of money, add a thyme infusion to the bath frequently. Place in a jar and keep in the home or at work for good luck.

Tonka Beans

The magickal uses include rituals and spells for love, wishes and is worn to gain prosperity and courage. Tonka beans are carried to give luck and protect from disease and/or to attract love. Promotes the success of your goals. Keep on your altar when performing love magick to enhance intent. When attending business discussions or job interviews, carry in a red flannel bag to attract good fortune and financial success. Considered to be a favorite hoodoo good luck charm to make wishes come true.

Valerian Root

Use for dream magick, sleep pillows, and sleep protection baths. Placed in charms and sachets for love and protection and used in. It is said that having Valerian root close will settle down a disagreement between couples. Keeping in the home or growing in a garden to will help in keeping harmony. It can be used to cleanse your ritual space. Very helpful in consecrating your incense burners. Wear to calm your emotions.

Vanilla

Use in love sachets, and wear the aromatic oil as an aphrodisiac. Magickal uses include love, lust, and passion. Strengthen mental abilities and revives your lost energy.

White Willow Bark

For love, protection, healing and divination. Carry and use in spells to attract love. Use the leaves, bark and wood in healing spells. Burn white willow bark with sandalwood to invoke spirits. Brings about blessings of the moon into your life and protects against negativity and evil energies.

Wolfsbane

The root or leaves may be burned as incense to banish prior energy from magickal blades and to fill it with protection. Make an infusion with the leaves or root for the same purpose and as a magickal wash for ritual tools or sacred space. To refresh the power of the knives, gather the fresh flowers of wolfsbane to make a tincture. Brings protection and magickal watchfulness against negative energies in ritual. Wash your new cauldron in the infusion or burn aconite in its first fire. Also used to invoke Hecate.

Note: Poisonous, do not ingest.

Wormwood

Used to remove anger, prevent violent acts, stop war, and for protection from the evil eye. Carry in your vehicle to protect from accidents especially on dangerous roads. Use as incense for clairvoyance, to summon spirits, or to enhance divinatory abilities. Can be sprinkled in the path of an enemy to bring them strife and misfortune (not recommended, remember the law of three).

Note: Can be poisonous, use with caution.

Yarrow Flower

Use to chase away depression, negative energy, prolonged sadness, or melancholy. When carried as an amulet or sachet it get rids of negative influences. Yarrow Flower also aids in divination. With a piece of parchment that you have written your fears, place yarrow in a yellow flannel bag carry with you to overcome them.

Yellow Dock

Used for abundance, healing and money. Sprinkle a potion of yellow dock about a place of your business to attract customers.

. . .

Ylang Ylang

To increase sexual attraction and influence. Also used for faery magick, peace, and love.

Yohimbe Bark

Yohimbe is used frequently in love and lust spells and cursing. It can also be used for empowering poppets. Use in sachets, ritual baths, spells, charms, mojo bags, magick powders, and incense blends. Also used in rituals of Pagan union.

Yucca

For change in self, protection and purification. Use an infusion of yucca to cleanse and purify the body before magick. Repeat this cleansing later if doing spells to remove hexes, curses, or illness. To remove jinxes and hexes rub a slice of yucca root all over your body once a day for seven days. It's said that a cross of yucca fiber located on the hearth protects your home from evil.

TEN

Herbal Spells

Dream Pillow

Items Needed:

- 4 tsp. Wormwood
- 4 tsp. Lavender
- 2 tsp. Chamomile flowers
- 2 tsp. Mugwort
- 1 tsp. Passion flower
- 1 tsp. Linden flowers and leaves
- 1 tsp. Marigold flowers
- 1 tsp. Rose petals
- 1 tsp. Cinquefoil
- 1 tsp. Elder flowers
- 1 tsp. Rosemary
- 1 tsp. Spearmint

Directions:

Sew up inside a small pillow approximately four by four or five by five inches and sleep on.

Astral Travel Pillow

Items Needed:
    3 tsp. Wormwood
    3 tsp. Vetiver
    2 tsp. Cedar
    1 tsp. Rose petals
    1 Tonka Bean, crushed
    1 pinch Orris Root
Directions:
Sew up inside a small pillow approximately four by four or five by five inches to promote astral travel during sleep

Good Luck Jar

To attract good fortune into your life, fill a jar with any combination of the magickal herbs:
    Items Needed:

Allspice	Buckthorn Bark
Chamomile	Clover
Dandelion	Fennel
Frankincense	Honeysuckle
Irish Moss	Job's Tears
High John the Conqueror	Lotus
Lucky Hand Root	Mistletoe
Mojo Wish Bean	Myrrh
Nutmeg	Orange
Peony Root	Poppy Seed
Rose Hips	Rosemary
Sacred Bark	Sandalwood
Spearmint	Star Anise
Thyme	Tonka Bean

Directions:

Seal the jar firmly and keep on a shelf or on a window sill in your kitchen on. Place your hands upon the jar each morning after you wake up and say:

"To the God and Goddess I do pray
Help guide me through another day
Let good fortune come now my way
Good luck comes here, now I say."

After repeating the chant, gently shake the jar a couple times. Kiss your jar prior to setting it back in its spot.

Anti-Theft Sachet

Items Needed:

2 tsp. Rosemary
1 tsp. Caraway seeds
1 tsp. Elder
1 tsp. Pine
1 pinch Garlic

Directions:

Tie herbs up in white cloth and hang over your front door to protect your house and its contents.

Healing Sachet

Items Needed:

2 tsp. Cinnamon
2 tsp. Sandalwood
1 tsp. Cayenne
1 tsp. Ginger
1 tsp. Rose petals
1 tsp. Rue

Directions:

Mix well and tie up in blue or purple cloth. Anoint sachet with Eucalyptus oil at each corner. Wear on your person or place close to your bed at night.

Wealth Sachet

Items Needed:
 2 tsp. Cinnamon
 2 tsp. Lemon Balm
 1 tsp. Cinquefoil
 1 tsp. Clove
 1 whole Tonka bean
 1 whole Vanilla bean
 Directions:
Crush the vanilla bean and mix all together. Give power to mixture. Tie up in a green or purple cloth. Carry with you to increase riches and to establish a positive cash flow.

Luck Incense

Items Needed:
 3 tsp. Allspice
 1 tsp. Star anise
 1 tsp. Fennel
 Burn on charcoal discs for luck.
 Lust Incense
 3 tsp. Patchouli
 2 tsp. Cinnamon
 2 tsp. Vanilla
 1 tsp. Lemongrass
 Directions:
 Burn on charcoal discs.

Herbal Protection Bath

Items Needed:
 Mint
 Lavender
 Rosemary

Rue

Fresh basil

A handful of salt

Directions:

Run a hot bath, and toss in all your herbs and the salt. Let the bath steep for a few minutes before getting in. Sit and soak for a while, visualizing that your body is picking up protective energy from all the herbs in the water.

When you're done, save some of the water and herbs in a bowl and toss outside.

Nine Herb Home Protection Talisman

Items Needed:

Glass jar with lid

½ cup Salt

Equal amounts of:

Dill

Sage

Anise

Black peppercorns

Garlic

Bay leaves

Basil

Fennel

Cloves

Directions:

This is an herbal talisman which will keep your home safe, both physically and astral. When you have mixed everything in the jar, put the lid on, shake the jar nine times, while saying:

Salt and herbs, nine times nine

Guard this home, this home of mine

These nine herbs have powerfully protective properties, along with salt, which is purifier. Keep the jar in the center of your home to protect it from all who would do it or you harm.

Prosperity Incense

Items Needed:

  2 tsp. Frankincense

  1 tsp. Cinnamon

  1 tsp. dried Lemon rind

  1 tsp. dried Orange rind

  1 tsp. Lemon Balm

Directions:

Burn charcoal discs to attract wealth

Conclusion

Wicca is not only about spells and full moon rituals; it is a broad practice that borders on many other methods. The Wiccan should be a magician, a farmer, a gardener, and a forager to understand more of the natural world on which our practice so heavily relies. Herbs are undoubtedly one of the greatest gifts from the Mother. The plants and botanicals breathe slowly with life and energy and offer themselves to us for our use. We are entitled to use these magickal plants, but we are also entrusted with the responsibility of being their voice and their guardian, making sure that they are not taken advantage of and abused. The pages that preceded this conclusion are full of the plants' wisdom, but your discovery journey does not end here. This is only a drop in the bu, and you have only dipped your toe into the nearly endless sea that is the use of herbs in magickal practice. We hope you have relearned a significant number of things from this book and that you will continue on your education journey and put what you have learned here and are still to learn into good practice. Always keep in mind our first law, "Eight words the Wiccan Rede fulfill, an it harm none do what ye will."

Blessed be!

About the Author

Monique Joiner Siedlak is a writer, witch, and warrior on a mission to awaken people to their greatest potential through the power of storytelling infused with mysticism, modern paganism, and new age spirituality. At the young age of 12, she began rigorously studying the fascinating philosophy of Wicca. By the time she was 20, she was self-initiated into the craft, and hasn't looked back ever since. To this day, she has authored over 40 books pertaining to the magick and mysteries of life.

To find out more about Monique Joiner Siedlak artistically, spiritually, and personally, feel free to visit her **official website**.

www.mojosiedlak.com

facebook.com/mojosiedlak

x.com/mojosiedlak

instagram.com/mojosiedlak

pinterest.com/mojosiedlak

bookbub.com/authors/monique-joiner-siedlak

African Spirituality Beliefs and Practices
Hoodoo
Seven African Powers: The Orishas
Cooking for the Orishas
Lucumi: The Ways of Santeria
Voodoo of Louisiana
Haitian Vodou
Orishas of Trinidad
Connecting with your Ancestors
Blood Magick
The Orishas
Vodun: West Africa's Spiritual Life
Marie Laveau: Life of a Voodoo Queen
Candomblé: Dancing for the God
Umbanda
Exploring the Rich and Diverse World

Divination Magic for Beginners
Divination with Runes
Divination with Diloggún
Divination with Osteomancy
Divination with the Tarot
Divination with Stones

The Beginner's Guide to Inner Growth
Astral Projection for Beginners
Meditation for Beginners
Reiki for Beginners

Mastering Your Inner Potential
Creative Visualization
Manifesting With the Law of Attraction

Holistic Healing and Energy
Healing Animals with Reiki

Crystal Healing
Communicating with Your Spirit Guides

Empathic Understanding and Enlightenment
Being an Empath Today

Life on Fire
Healing Your Inner Child
Change Your Life
Raising Your Vibe

The Indie Author's Guides
The Indie Author's Guide to Fast Drafting Your Novel

Get a Handle on Life
Get a Handle on Stress
Time Bound
Get a Handle on Anxiety
Get a Handle on Depression
Get a Handle on Procrastination

The Holistic Yoga and Wellness Series
Yoga for Beginners
Yoga for Stress
Yoga for Back Pain
Yoga for Weight Loss
Yoga for Flexibility
Yoga for Advanced Beginners
Yoga for Fitness
Yoga for Runners
Yoga for Energy
Yoga for Your Sex Life
Yoga to Beat Depression and Anxiety
Yoga for Menstruation
Yoga to Detox Your Body

More Books by Monique

Yoga to Tone Your Body

The DIY Body Care Series

Creating Your Own Body Butter
Creating Your Own Body Scrub
Creating Your Own Body Spray

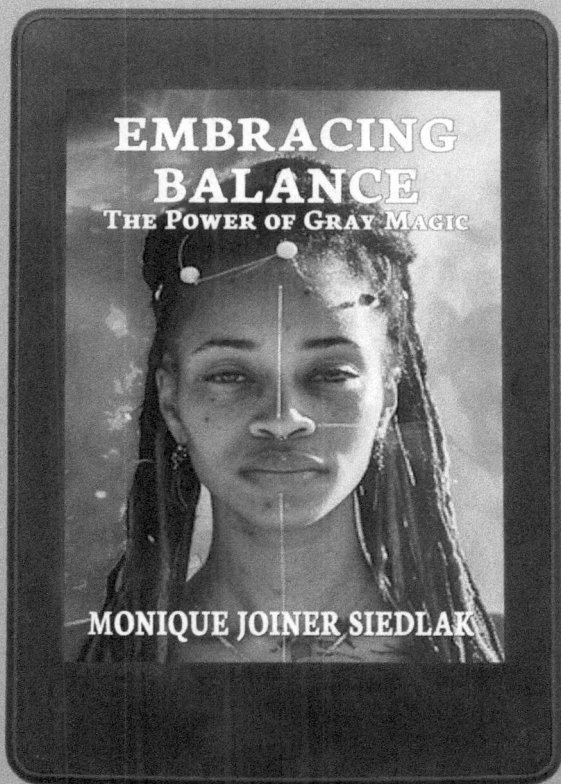

WANT TO BE
FIRST TO KNOW?

EMBRACING
BALANCE
The Power of Gray Magic

MONIQUE JOINER SIEDLAK

JOIN MY NEWSLETTER!
WWW.MOJOSIEDLAK.COM/MOONLIGHT-MUSINGS

SUPPORT ME BY LEAVING A REVIEW!

goodreads

amazon

BookBub

Download on
Apple Books

GET IT ON
Google Play

nook
by Barnes & Noble

Rakuten
kobo

www.ingramcontent.com/pod-product-compliance
Lightning Source LLC
Chambersburg PA
CBHW071626040426
42452CB00009B/1501